Contents

1

<u>War</u>

Your mind is the battlefield,
Every seeds of war sprouted here.
It is between the two things,
Devine and evil,
Good and bad,
Success and failure,
Happiness and sorrow,
It is the war of your inner feelings.
It is never ending struggle.
It is your lone war. But you've to fight.
You've to come out.
You've to regain your lost kingdom of peace.
You've to liberate yourself from this war.

.......****.....

2

<u>Life is full of Mysteries</u>

Life is full of mysteries,
Sometimes it shows you green trees,
Invites you with its delicious fruits,
And sometimes it gets off with its bitter fluids.
Life gives you full of surprises,
Sometimes it gives you beautiful prizes.
It shows you lovely images,
And sometimes it shows you fake mirages.
In life, both happiness and sorrow

Come one after another in a row.
Life is for a moment,
Full of lament.
When it says goodbye,
When everything remains lie,
When it stops its flow,
You don't know.
What will go to happen with you?
Now, today and tomorrow,
You don't know anything.
But every moment you're heading towards its destiny,
It's the reality.
Life is always uncertain,
It's an ordinary curtain.
How many houses you've built;
How many lives you've heal;
It only counts.
Who'll go to remember you?
Who'll go to forget you?
It doesn't matter.
How long you've spent your life in this world,
It doesn't matter.
But how you've spent your life in this world,
It does matter.
Before anything going too late,
Open your life's gate.
Do something great,
So that someday, somebody reminds your name after your death.

Life is Beautiful

Life is beautiful,
You can make it more beautiful.
Everything is in your hands.
What do you want in your life?
It's up to you
Whether you want your life in the heaven
Or in the hell.
Both Earth and Heaven is within your reach.

It's up to you
Whether you want your life in the garden of flowers
Or in the land of weeds.
Whether you want a sand stone
Or a gem stone.
It's in your hands.
Life is like day and night,
Every day is a new dawn and a new dusk.
Sometime life is like a fading autumn,
And sometime life is like a blooming spring.
It's the reality of life.
You must accept it!
But you can't escape from it,
It's the law of life.
Try to taste the spirit of every season of your life,
And spread its beauty everywhere.
If you ever can't build a grand mansion.
Then what!
You can build a house of love.
If you ever can't live a life of luxury.
Then what!
You can live a life of happiness.
Love your life,
Love your fellow mates,
Give them the sweet flavor of your life.
Life is a journey of one time.
You don't know the journey of another world.
Whatever you have
Everything is right now.
So, live the life of every moment,
And make it more meaningful and beautiful.
Our journey of life
Our journey of life,
Begins with our first breath,
Ends with our last breath.
We find our natives,
We get our relatives.

We have to leave one day,
But, nobody can't say.
Our life is a drama of uncertainties.
The ends with the fall of curtain.
Every moment of this life is precious for us,
Every day is a day of bonus.
We all are travelers,
Nobody is permanent dwellers.
So, never hurt anybody.
Despite you get hurt.
Give love,
Receive love.
It is a life full of sorrow.
It is a life full of joy,
Like day and night.
Learn to laugh,
Learn to weep.
But as long as you survive,
Always try to revive,
Because it is our journey of life.

......****.....

3

Your vision

What you want to do be?
What you want to see?
Everything depends upon your vision.
Find out your reason.
Every event of life is matters to you,
And it asks you its demand,

You must know the right command.
Guide yourself in the wide direction,
To succeed in your mission.
Know your inner potential, which is unlimited,
Don't spend your life like a timid.
Open your mind, which you keep lock,
It's time to unlock.
Wash your unclean eyes,
Wear out your old fashion,
Try to be wise.
Everything, which is unseen,
Now, it is visible.
It is your time to walk,
To get your golden luck.
Visualize your ideas to the world,
So that you can shine like a diamond.

......****.....

4

<u>Only you can change yourself!</u>

Change yourself,
Change is the universal law.
You want change in your life,
It may be from good to better
And from better to best.
But you can't change yourself,
Still you remain unchanged.
You can't change your mind,
Because your thoughts are clashed with you,
Even though your principle doesn't allow you.
You can't change your heart,
Because your emotions are attached with you,
Even though your conscience doesn't allow you.
You can't change your life ,
Because you love the way you're living,
Even though your desires and wishes are heated on the burning coal.

You can't change your world,
Because you like the way you're dwelling,
Even though your life is hurting in the bushes of thorns.
Ask yourself- Is it my life the way I'm surviving?
Try to figure out your answers of your life.
Why are you committing self-destruction?
You've right to live a better life in this world.
Nobody can snatch from you.
Life is to live,
But not to die before your death.
Why are you hesitated?
Stop your self-haunted life.
Come out from your dark cell of dilemma.
Feel the fresh air of this beautiful world.
They are calling you.
You need change.
It's true that you can't bring hundred percent change in your life,
At least you can bring one percent change in your life.
If you ever can't get the ocean of water,
Then what!
At least you can get few drops of rainwater.
Nobody can change you.
Only you can change yourself.
Time
Time has a wing,
Which is always swinging.
It is never lie,
It is ever flying.
It is so fast,
And never long last.
It is unmatched,
So, nobody can catch.
Once it'll fly away,
You'll never get another chance to see its way.
If it'll lost,
You've to pay heavy cost.
......****.....

5

<u>A Heart of Mine</u>

A heart of mine
in a long lifeline.
I've a lot of hope,
And a thirst of love.
Sometime, I felt a heart alone,
And living in unknown.
Hurt by a spine,
Which wounded my desire
And set it into fire.
But, I'm not getting tire,
Because, God blesses His stir.
He tied me in His love wire,
And I couldn't get retire,
He changed my entire human's attire.

......****.....

6

<u>A Game</u>

My life is like a game,
It has many names.
I was caught by the hands of dame,
And she took away my fame.
My face felt ashamed,
And my legs turned lame;
I was like her tame.
Who will get rid of me?

Only my Heaven knows!
My life lost its aim.

......****.....

7

<u>Human's Life</u>

Born as a child,
Fall in mother's lap.
He never be alone,
Meets his fellow mates,
And bind in the native bonds.
Grown as a young,
He is desirous to earn,
Whatever he wished;
Tried to succeed,
Forgot his moralities,
And met miseries and sorrows.
As an old,
He thinks and realized.
His cultures and character shows,
His life span,
His noble deeds,
Makes him great
His life is for a day
End with death.

......****.....

8

<u>A Drama</u>

Our life is a drama,
Without rehearsal;
Where, I, thou, and we,
To act and play the role.
An actor and an actress as a whole;
On the stage of earth.
Our life is a drama,
As the curtain rises, it begins.
The story full of mysteries,
Woes and tears be the emotions,
Jokes and laughs be the funs,
Praises and criticisms are the rewards.
Our life is a drama,
The rich or the poor; the king or the beggar,
Be the characters.
But, each part got its significance,
The few get
Special appearance;
The few remains as the glittering stones,
And a few ever shines as the shining stars.

......****.....

9

<u>Plan</u>

It's a golden rule,
It's an old rule,
Which makes the life in control,
And makes the man in good role.
It's a routine,
Changes our lifeline.

It's a chart,
Which visualize our part.
It reflecting our future,
And effecting our nature.
It moves the life in order,
And makes the man in proper.
It's a plan which change the life of man.

......****.....

10

<u>Longevity</u>

It's all about uncertainties;
No one could say,
Neither foreteller nor astrologer.
It's the life,
Which is neither short nor prolong,
Neither fix nor long.
It's depending upon its own;
An unsolved puzzle;
It's the longevity of unknown,
And makes the life dazzle.
It has initial point,
But has no final point.
It has entry door,
But has no exit door.
Some live long life,
Some live short life.
It's the tragedy of life.
It comes to the end at any time,

So, leave some remarkable thing.
It's the longevity of life,
So, leave some valuable thing.

......****.....

11

<u>Desire</u>

It's your desire,
Like the fire.
It burn,
So, try to learn.
Whatever you did mistake,
Try to retake.
Don't be too late,
In your way to make.
It's your life.
Keep it safe,
Try to fly,
As much as you can, high.
Hold your heart to fight,
For your own right.
Then you'll be the star of the sky,
You'll ever shine in the above sky.

......****.....

12

<u>Mind</u>

It's full of might,
You've to guide.

It's unique.
It reaches the highest zenith.
It is faster than the wind.
It helps to win.
It is the main centre,
Allow your heart and soul to enter.
It is the host,
Don't try to lost.
It is the power of infinite,
Set your goal in definite.
It is the source of energy; extract,
Turn your new ideas; exact.
Concentrate in the right incident,
To build your confident.
You've to ignite it,
In order to get your bright light in it.
Don't make it nomad,
Else, you'll become mad.
You need to direct,
To raise it erects.

It is your mind the main cause,
Which you can't pause.
Only you can tame,
Then you get your fame.

.......****.....

13

<u>Conscience</u>

Lying in your heart's deep,
Nobody is daring to peep.
It is always thinking,
You're in the touch of linking.
It ever modify,
To cleanse your mind and to purify.
It constantly extracts,
To turn you into the form of exact.
Every time it reacts,
And tells you to act.
Your mind may cheat,
But, it honestly heed .
It stands in your way to guide,
To show you the path of light.
Nobody can observe you, but its eyes judge,
And you're under watch.
Whatever may be the condition, it grasp to control,
And it plays an important role.
It is none other than your own voice of soul,
Try to listen it and to hold.

......****.....

14

<u>Patience</u>

A rope, which is tight,
Always binds you with might.
It moves slowly,
But, always non-stop flow.
It doesn't allow you to be haste,
And stops you from waste.

It teaches you the best lesson,
Which is never ending moral of session.
It helps you to take your decision free,
So that you can widely see.
Its taste is bitter,
But, its result makes you better.
It acts as your true friend,
One who is wholly trained.
In your every agony of trouble,
It makes you stable.
You can stand like the rock,
And nobody ever try to stroke.
It is your patience,
Make it you priceless essence.

……****…..

15

<u>Thought</u>

Every thought that comes to you,
Always affects you.
Your inner image,
Your outer image,
All are reflects on you,
Without it nobody can live.
Because, it's the art of living.
Whether you're right or you're wrong,
Whether you're weak or you're strong.
You're merely a medium of reaction,
But, all are guided by its action.
It becomes wild, when it is not properly tame,
Your ways of life become lame.
Before, it'll get dirt and turn impure,
And spoil you, make it pure.

16

<u>Attitude</u>

Our life is all about attitude,
Lift us to the greatest altitude.
It boost our might,
And helps us to reach the topmost height.
It raises our inner power of will,
And make us like the giant hill.
Flows the energy of charm,
And hold our weak arm.
Our heart never fall,
And there is no doubts of call.
We could see the lightning in the darkness,
And our life starts dancing in the brightness.
Our life become bold and tall head,
And we ever ready to march ahead.

17

<u>Luck</u>

Your destiny is long,
So, tune your heroic song.
It is full of sharp nail,

Ever stand to fail.
But, you've nothing to mourn,
Sound your alarm horn.
Whatever your peer says,
Wherever they direct your ways,
And whatever you've seen,
Forget it and keep your keen.
Keep your eyes in the right act,
And try to search your tact.
If your steps are, slow,
There is nothing to blow.
Don't worry!
Don't feel sorry!
Hold your vibrating nerve,
And control your crave.
If you ever fail to bounce,
But, never give up pouncing.
When you begin your walk,
You'll surely get your luck.

......****.....

18

<u>Golden Ray</u>

O Losing and weak heart!
Why you're wasting your valuable birth?
You haven't seen the sparkling gem,
How much it resists the stresses and the burning flame.
Then only it Trans form into a new shape,
And all likes to have.
Why not you see the clear sky?
Open your clouded eyes to view high.
Look at the king of air,
The Eagle, which always fly so high with dare,
Try to be like the king of jungle,
Who walk lonely, but nobody try to mingle.

Why you're trapping yourself in self- made illusion of net?
Set a new target.
Come out!
Stop it!
Why you're keeping nail on your own way?
Create a new horizon for your own golden ray.

......****.....

19

<u>Respect</u>

Whoever he is?
Whoever she is?
Open your heart to respect,
And keep your expect.
It is the warm gratitude,
Express your attitude.
Whether senior
Or junior.
As you, greet,
As you, get treat.
It is your manner,
Which tells about you, what you've learnt from your elder.
If your head is bow,
You don't become low,
But, your happiness adds,
And you'll feel glad.
We're civilize man,
We're not savage.
Even the beast know,
How to show?
If your parents are old,
Then they are your valuable gold.
Don't feel shame,

You should respect them.
Pay your homage,
To brighten their image,
It is your merit,
Which you inherit,
Because when you earn,
Then only you can return.
When you follow,
You become a good fellow.
It turns you great,
And you get your real mate.

......****.....

20

Wicket Habit

In the beginning, it is very sweet,
Later it'll start haunting you and it'll become difficult to quit.
It binds you with the fencing of string,
And you will trap in its hanging link.
Once you'll involve,
You'll totally dissolve.
You'll become heavy,
And your life will flow in wavy.
Your pious life will adulterate,

Your thoughts will slowly penetrate.
It'll tie you in its dark cave,
And you will not move your pave.
It is like the deep ditch,
Where you'll ever meet hitch.
If you'll become its slave,
You'll get hard slap.
It is like a gum,
Make your mind dumb.
Everything will go to stick,
And nothing will come in your pick.
It will form like a thick layer,
And every time it'll wear.
It is like the water with oil,
Your purity will spoil.
It'll weaken your ability,
And ruin your quality.
So , don't swim in the shallow sea !
Don't spend like the life of hollow tree.
Take a close look,
In order to catch it with your hook.

......****.....

<u>Anger</u>

It is the anger,
Very danger.
It is like a burning fire,
Gives you a sweating tire,
It burn your heart,
It burns your art.
It is very hot,
Burn you a lot.
So, never try to ignite,
Because you'll get bite, whenever you invite.
It is an inflammable flame,
Its flying ashes make you blind.
Your valuable energy will lose,
It quickly lessens your mental boost.
It is like a dose of poison for your health,
Always melt.
It is a dangerous temper,
All are badly hamper.
It leads your life in to the path of hell,
So, don't dig your own death of well.
Before, it is going to block,
And give you a heavy dock.
Try to find out its real cause,
So that, you can pause.

22

<u>Jealous</u>

Why you allow growing this weed?
Don't sow its dispersing seed.
If others are in adorable cloth,
Why you ought to spoil their worth?
If you don't know, how to admire!
You've no right to despair.
It is their fortune,

Why do you see their misfortune?
They are your peer,
You ought to cheer.
How do you feel?
When you dine the untidy meal,
It's like a poisoning pill,
Open its mouth to kill.
It makes your mind dirty,
And create tension in your unity.
Everything is earn by good deed,
It's the duty of all human creeds.
It sprouts the sin for other,
Fear from Godfather.
He loves all,
Because, you're His eternal soul.

When He close His blessing eyes,
You ever revolve in this mortal dice.
So, fill your heart with pious,
And put-off this flames of jealous.

…….****…..

23

<u>Falsehood</u>

When you make someone fool,
You feel cool.
But, it'll chase you,
To catch you,
And it put you into the jail,
Where is full of nail.
There is no shinning of sun,
And you can't run.
It is the venom of arrow,
Strike your heart in barrow.
If you ever try to hide the truth,
You never get good fruit.
How long you'll keep enclose?
Someday it'll disclose.
It is a sin,
You must win!
You wanted to sell.
And spend your life in dreadful dale?
You know!
Yes or no.
The culprit of evil,
Is one-day reveal.
If you want to bind the mutual brotherhood,
Then, you must leave the habit of falsehood.

24

<u>Insult</u>

Whenever you'll get insulted,
Don't be disheartened, but wait for a big result.
If yours fellow mates make fun,
And trigger their laughing gun,
Even then, try to keep busy,

And try to move easy.
Control your opening mouth,
And stop your angry shout.
Work for goodwill,
Believe in your powerful will,
Don't take as their cursing,
But, accept as their blessing.
They are as your mentor,
Help you to become a good actor.
So, give as your examination,
Show them your determination.

......****.....

25

Relationship

It is as soft as cotton string,
Which ever need strong ring?
When it'll going to break,
How it'll get crack,
Nobody know its secret shots,
So, bind it with tight knot.
Once our mutual faith will lost,
We've to pay its heavy cost.
We'll suffocate all alone,
And we can't scream to call anyone.
Like no one could ever write anything on the beach of sand,
Because, it'll soon wash away by the tides' hand.
Stand together,
Sail further,
To the next shore,
We need our touching core.
But, if we divide ourselves,

We all drown into the sea depth.
Our bond is only match with love,
But, not with the faded hope.
We could live in this world,
When we learn how to hug all.

…….****…..

26

<u>Bad Memories</u>

From your bad memories,
You'll only get the bag of worries.
It makes you cry,
And force you to die.
It'll turn your life haunted,
And you'll become faint hearted.
Everything will appear dark,
Everything will become your task.
So, stop your waves of flowing tears,
Don't be the victim of fears.
It'll block your success path,
And your doors of life will remain shut.
If you want to go beyond,
Then decide your own horizon.
Forget your dreadful past,
Nothing will long last.
When you'll learn to live again,
Then only you'll forget your pain.

…….****…..

27

<u>Face</u>

If you've an ugly face,
It'll not the main case.
But, your true heart,
And your right birth.
If anybody hate...!
Then, they will never be your genuine mate.
It's your sweet voice,
Make you the best choice.
If they will laugh at you,
And try to turn down your view.
Even, don't look down,
But try to be the great crown.
Always be sure,
And try to live in pure....
Be a wise!
Be a nice!
One day you'll see through your eyes,
These people will come to you.
And when will you get great luck,
They will hug you.

......****.....

28

<u>Smile</u>

It's your melodious smile,
Spread from the mile.
It attracts very near,
And makes very dear.
It is like the blooming flower,
Splash the pleasant of shower.
It is a song, which is sweet,
Ever ready to meet,
It is the fragrance of perfumes,
You feel the joy and the colors of fumes.

Your dusty journey of life become easy,
And brings you full of cozy.
It is your inner feelings which is visible in your eyes,
Where your hidden happiness is lies.
You feel its chill,
And your faded life will dance with thrill.
It is your soft smile,
Not for a while.
It is your gifted jewel of nature,
Try to wear in your every juncture.

......****.....

29

<u>Shyness</u>

Why do you feel shy?
If there is nothing, lie.
Ne'er hesitate to say,
Speak up whatever is lay.
Look at the glorious Sun's ray,
Nobody will dare to stop his ways.
If the Moon cover her elegance,
Then who will praise her glance!
The sweet flowers is soon dry-up,
Like the hopeless life is soon fed-up.
A fruit without taste,
Is like the useless peels of waste.
If you hide your natural talent,
Then nobody will know yours intelligent.
It is your puzzling doubt,
Like the covering cloud.
Come out!
Take out!
Work for good,
And change your mood.

It is the act of silly,
You can't feed your hungry belly.

…...****…..

30

<u>Not everything is for us</u>

Everything that comes in our mind,
Is not always suitable for us.
Everything that we feel in our heart,
Is not always pleasant for us.
Everything that we see with our eyes,
Is not always visible for us.
Everything that we hear with our ears,
Is not always true for us.
Everything that we smell with our nose,
Is not always sweet for us.
Everything that we taste with our tongue,
Is not always delicious for us.
Everything that we speak with our mouth,
Is not always correct for us.
Everything that we smile with our lips,
Is not always enjoyable for us.
Everything that we touch with our hands,
Is not always tender for us.
Everything that we desire in life,
Is not for us.

…....****…..

31

<u>The Right way</u>

Follow the right way,
See the lighting ray,

Keep this as your target,
And whatever you did in the past, just forget.
Pace your move in forward,
Never see backward.
Learn to tackle the situation,
With bold heart and action.
Do what is essential,
With your potential.
Turn your life into a new shape,
Know its beauty and keep everything safe.

......****.....

32

Light

Where there is light, there is life.
Where there is light, there is love.
Where there is light, there is peace.
Where there is light, there is happiness.
Where there is light, there is goodness.
Where there is light, there is blessing.
Where there is light, there is power.
Where there is light, there is energy.
Where there is light, there is knowledge.
Where there is light, there is wisdom.
Where there is light, there is divine.
Where there is light, there is serenity.
Where there is light, there is vision
Where there is light, there is holiness.
Where there is light, there is salvation.

Where there is light, there is everything.
Where there is no light, there is only 'death'.

......****.....

33

<u>Your Nature</u>

Your physical appearance,
Is for a time being.
It'll perish with time.
Your infinite mind,
Is a source of power.
It'll clean with nice thoughts.
Your beautiful heart,
Is a core of love.
It'll fill with compassion.
Your twin eyes,
Is not to wear the lens of proud,
It'll tire with age.
Your dimple cheek,
Is not to wink.
It'll wrinkle with years.
Your pink lips,
Is to smile sweet.
It'll dry-up with season.
Your delicious tongue,
Is not to swing the sarcastic words.
It'll become tasteless with bitterness.
Your golden character,
Is to polish the virtues.
It'll speak-up your true nature.

......****.....

34

<u>Meanings of Life</u>

Look at the blue Sky!
Look at the bright Sun!
Look at the shinning Moon!
Look at the twinkling Stars!
Look at the flying Clouds!
Then compare...
The Earth,
The Ocean,
The high peak mountains,
The flowing rivers,
The falling streams,
The green trees,
The herd of animals,
The flying birds,
The blooming flowers,
The humming bees,
The colorful butterflies,
Finally compare with yourself..........
Then you know the true meanings of your life.

…....****…...

35

<u>Laziness</u>

It is your laziness,
Corrodes and wear you.
You become like the useless metal.
It is your laziness,
Spread you dirt.
You become like the stagnant water.

It is your laziness,
Cover you with dust.
You become like barren soil.
It is your laziness,
Make you untidy.
You become like the dirty clothes.
It is your laziness,
Eat you blindly.
You become like the hollow tree.
It is your laziness,
Kill you slowly.
You become its prey.

......****.....

36

<u>Idle Mind</u>

Your life is beautiful.
Live with joy.
It'll become hell,
If you make your mind idle.
Your life is beautiful.
Live with healthy and wealthy.
It'll become sick,
If you make your mind idle.
Your life is beautiful.
Live with your deeds.
It'll become ruin,
If you make your mind idle.
Your life is beautiful.
Live with your great ideas.
It'll become lifeless,
If you make your mind idle.

Your life is beautiful.
Live with your qualities.
It'll become meaningless,
If you make your mind idle.

......****.....

37

<u>Your Task!</u>

If your task is to touch the sky,
You must overcome its limit.
If every time you're thrown,
You've to fly again.
If your task is to cross the ocean,
You must overcome its tides.
If every time you're drowned,
You've to swim again.
If your task is to climb the mountain,
You must overcome its height.
If every time you're fallen,
You've to get up again.
If your task is to win the battle,
You must overcome your weakness.
If every time you're defeated,
You've to fight back again.
If your task is to complete the race,
You must overcome the tough opponent.
If every time you're beaten,
You've to run again.

......****.....

38

<u>The Greatness</u>

The greatness of Earth,
Lies in her life giving blessings.
The greatness of Sky,
Lies in its vastness.
The greatness of Ocean,
Lies in its deepness.
The greatness of Sun,
Lies in its brightness.
The greatness of Moon,
Lies in its dimness.
The greatness of River,
Lies in its cleanliness.
The greatness of Trees,
Lies in its greenery.
The greatness of Forest,
Lies in its thickness.
The greatness of Flower,
Lies in its fragrance.
The greatness of Fruit,
Lies in its taste.
The greatness of Birds,
Lies in their sweetness.

The greatness of Animals,
Lies in their unity.
The greatness of Man,
Lies in his good deeds.

......****.....

<u>Give and Take</u>

Our life is all about:
Give and take.
If you give love,
In return, you'll get love.
Our life is all about:
Give and take.
If you give hatred,
In return, you'll get hatred.
Our life is all about:
Give and take.
If you give happiness,
In return, you'll get happiness.
Our life is all about:
Give and take,
If you give smile,
In return, you'll get smile.
Our life is all about:
Give and take.
If you give tears,
In return, you'll get tears.
Our life is all about:
Give and take.
If you give blessing,
In return, you'll get blessing.
Our life is all about:
Give and take.
If you give curse,
In return, you'll get curse.

.......****.....

<u>Experiences of Life</u>

We don't feel,
The joy of laugh,
If we never shed tears in life.
We don't feel,
The gift of love,
If we never give love in life.
We don't feel,
The pains of others,
If we never get hurt in life.
We don't feel,
The heat of sun,
If we never get wet in the rain.
We don't feel,
The brightness of light,
If we never spend in the darkness.
We don't feel,
The current of water.
If we never dive in the sea.
We don't feel,
The taste of food,
If we never get starve in life.
We don't feel,
The sweetness of water,
If we never get thirst in life.
We don't feel,
The shivering of cold,
If we never get sweat in life.
We don't feel,
The softness of snow,
If we never land on the dry sand.
We don't feel,
The fragrance of flower,
If we never get the smell of foul.

We don't feel,
The peace of loneliness,
If we never spend in the crowd.
We don't feel,
The excitement of success,
If we never fail in life.
We don't feel,
The beauties of life,
If we never get the experiences of life.

......****.....

41

<u>Obstacles</u>

It was the strong wind, which attacked me.
I didn't see.
How those uncertain troubles came on my way?
I didn't get time to realize on that day.
I blown away in the unknown place,
I couldn't replace.
I got a mighty blow.
It was very hard and made me very slow.
My days of life was tough,
I had no dare to rise up.
When I opened my dull eyes,
I saw the glowing sun, which turned into a big size.
He said something to me,
I heard his voice.
He asked me to stand and fight.
Then I found my self-belief,

I felt relief.
I re-discovered myself,
I dare to face the challenges without any help.
It was my great move,
It was the obstacles, which taught me how to tackle.

......****.....

42

<u>Virtues</u>

The Flower never tells its virtue.
But, its fragrance and sweetness,
Attracts the bees to come in it.
The Tree never tells its virtue.
But, its fruits and thick leaves,
Attracts the birds to make shelter in it.
The Forest never tell its virtue,
But, its evergreen and life giving boons,
Attracts the animals to dwell in it.
The River never tells its virtue.
But, its water resources,
Attracts the aquatic lives to live in it.
The Mountain never tells its virtue.
But, its steepness and great height,
Attracts the adventurous mind to climb in it.
The Ocean never tells its virtue.
But, its vastness and deepness,
Attracts the explorers to explore in it,
The Great man never tells his virtue.
But, his great deeds,
Attracts the people to follow him.

......****.....

43

Inner-Self

When you're lonely,
Who is speaking to you?
It's your inner-self,
It is your companion.
When you're lonely,
Who is guiding you?
It's your inner-self,
It is your conscience.
When you're lonely,
Who is hoping for you?
It's your inner-self,
It is your optimism.
When you're lonely,
Who is demoralizing you?
It's your inner-self,
It is your pessimism.
When you're lonely,
Who is fighting for you?
It's your inner-self,
It is your egoism.
When you're lonely,
Who is crying for you?
It's your inner-self,
It is your realization.
When you're lonely,
Who is laughing at you?
It's your inner-self,
It is your foolishness.
When you're lonely,
Who is disturbing you?
It's your inner-self,
It is your old memories.
When you're lonely,
Who is inspiring you?
It's your inner-self,

It is your faith.
When you're lonely,
Who is living with you?
It's your inner-self,
It is your thought.
When you're lonely,
Who is singing inside you?
It's your inner-self,
It is your love.
When you're lonely,
Who is dreaming for you?
It's your inner-self,
It is your expectation.
When you're lonely,
Who is playing with you?
It's your inner-self,
It's childish in you.
When you're lonely,
Who is sleeping with you?
It's your inner-self,
It is your peacefulness.
When you're lonely,
Who loves you?
It's your inner-self,
It is your core of heart.
When you're lonely,
Who is spying you?
It's your inner-self,
It guards you from evils.
When you're lonely,
Who is with you?
It's your inner-self,
It is always with you.

......****.....

44

<u>To Get Our Living</u>

The seasons are always changing.
They never stop.
The sun is always shinning.
It never stops.
The stars are always twinkling.
They never stop.
The wind is always blowing.
It never stops.
The river is always flowing.
It never stops.
The stream is always falling.
It never stops.
The trees are always growing.
They never stop.
The flowers are always blooming.
They never stop.
The birds are always flying.
They never stop.
The animals are always grazing.
They never stop.
The ants are always working.
They never stop.
These are the laws of nature,
They never stop.

45

<u>Your Questions!</u>

What is this World?
This World is your battlefield.
Who are you?
You're the lone warrior.
Who are your enemies?

Your enemies are:
Lust,
Attachment,
Ego,
Greed,
And anger.
How could you face them?
You could face them with:
Patience,
Intellect,
Purity,
Compassion,
And love.
Who are challenging with you?
It's your own: desires and attachments.
Who is your best friend?
It's your conscience.

......****.....

46

<u>Ask yourself</u>

When your heart is fill with hatred,
Then ask yourself- WHY?
Tell your heart to love.
When your heart is fill with jealousy,
Then ask yourself- WHY?
Tell your heart to be generous.
When your heart is fill with cruelties,
Then ask yourself- WHY?
Tell your heart to give mercy.
When your heart is fill with anger,
Then ask yourself- WHY?
Tell your heart to remain peace.
When your heart is fill with evils,
Then ask yourself- WHY?

Tell your heart to maintain divinity.
When your heart is fill with worry,
Then ask yourself- WHY?
Tell your heart to be merry.
When your heart is fill with negative,
Then ask yourself- WHY?
Tell your heart to be positive.

.....****.....

47

<u>Parts of our Life</u>

Life has two parts:
Birth and death
Love and hatred
Happiness and unhappiness
Sweetness and bitterness
Success and failure
Day and night
Brightness and darkness
Company and lonely
But, we've to live,
These are the parts our life.

......****.....

48

<u>Failures</u>

Failure is only a momentary,
It's a temporary.
No doubt, it bends your road,
But it can't block your road.
Even success is not permanent,
You need your temperament.
Your hope is your golden ray,
Show you your hidden way.
Don't cry,
Never say die.
Believe yourself,
Work yourself.
Try to get up!
Try to rise up!
Don't make your heart weak,
Make your heart strong.
When you turn your failure into success,
Then you'll definitely get your success.
Never mind failure,
Your failure is the stepping-stone,
Which leads you to the ultimate milestone.

......****.....

49

Better Way

It's always better way,
To change the direction of wind,
If it is blowing violently towards you,
Rather than waiting to blown away.
It's always better way,
To change the route of water,
If it is flowing turbulently towards you,
Rather than waiting to drawn into.
It's always better way,

To change the path of smoking fire,
If it is polluting the air towards you,
Rather than waiting to suffocate in it.
It's always better way,
To change the arising situation,
If it is disturbing your life,
Rather than waiting to die within.

......****.....

50

<u>Today and Yesterday</u>

Whoever you're today,
Whatever you're today,
Wherever you're today,
This is significant for you.
Whoever you were yesterday,
Whatever you were yesterday,
Wherever you were yesterday,
That is not significant for you.
Whatever you're thinking today,
Whatever you're working today,
Whatever you're getting today,
Wherever you're going today,
This is significant for you.
Whatever you were thinking yesterday,
Whatever you were working yesterday,
Whatever you were getting yesterday,
Wherever you were going yesterday,
That is not significant for you.
Everything is depends upon today.
Nothing is depends upon yesterday.

So, forget yesterday,
And work today.

......****.....

51

<u>If You Are......</u>

If you're a thinker,
And if you can!
Give the meanings of life,
To the dying mind.
If you're a philosopher,
And if you can!
Advice the importance of life.
To the dying soul.
If you're a writer,
And if you can!
Write the experiences of life,
To the lives.
If you're a teacher,
And if you can!
Teach the lessons of life ,
To the dying heart.
If you're an explorer,
And if you can!
Inspire the adventures of life,
To the dying nerve.
If you're an inventor,
And if you can!
Present the fascinations of life,
To the dying hands.
If you're a discoverer,
And if you can!
Visualize the mysteries of life,
To the dying eyes.
If you're a healer,

And if you can!
Bless the pleasures of life,
To the dying health.
If you're a builder,
And if you can!
Build the treasures of life,
To the dying head.
If you're a musician,
And if you can!
Compose the music of life,
To the dying voice.
If you're a singer,
And if you can!
Sing the songs of life,
To the dying love.
If you're an artist,
And if you can!
Paint the colors of life,
To the dying man.
If you're a simple man,
And if you can!
Mould your simple life,
To live a happy life.

......****.....
52

Silent Sleep

Don't resign so early,
From this life.
Never say good-bye.
You've to do many things,
For yourself and for your beloved ones.
If you want to earn,
You must learn.
If you want to receive something,

Then first, you've to give something.
Lead yourself; lead everyone.
Do your own deeds.
Live your life for noble cause,
And serve the life of needy.
Guide your footprint,
To the world before you going to silent sleep.

......****.....

53

<u>Accept You!</u>

In this world, no one is yours,
All are own self.
Everything is your own.
Who is yours?
Who are others?
You can't say.
Who are your friends?
Who are your enemies?
You can't deny.
The warning bell tells you,
The tales of smiling and weeping.
Your life is not run by anybody,
But, with yourself.
There is no one,
Only accept you.

......****.....

54

Disguise

We're wearing an ordinary dress.
Everything is in His hands.
Whether man or woman,
Whether birds or animals,
Everything is His creations.
We all are living beings,
Living for a time being.
Try to become like a sage,
But never try to become like a savage.
Try to pass your loving kiss,
But never try to pass your poisonous hiss.
Leave your natures of cat,
Leave the life of rat.
Your life is not to sting,
But to live the life of king.
Life is full of hard task,
Wear out your devil's mask.
Don't live in disguise,
Come out from your dark cell.
Live the life of noble,
And try to become the crown of global.

……****…..

55

Your Fight

You've to fight for good,
But, not for bad.
You've to fight for right,
But, not for wrong.
You've to fight with love,

But, not with hatred.
You've to fight with divinity,
But' not with evil.
You've to fight with your egos,
But, not with your life.
You've to fight with yourself,
But, not with others.
You're the lone soldier in your fight,
So, fight with your full might.

......****.....

56

<u>Your Thoughts</u>

If your thoughts are strong,
You feel strong.
If your thoughts are weak,
You feel weak.
If your thoughts are positive,
You feel positive.
If your thoughts are negative,
You feel negative.
If your thoughts are good,
You feel good.
If your thoughts are bad,
You feel bad.
If your thoughts are right,
You feel right.
If your thoughts are wrong,
You feel wrong.
If your thoughts are great,

You feel great.
If your thoughts are small,
You feel small.
Everything is all about your thoughts.
You're rule by own thoughts.

......****.....

57

<u>Think !</u>

If there is no sun in the sky,
Think !
What will happen?
There will be only darkness everywhere.
If there is no Moon in the sky,
Think !
What will happen?
The sky will become ugly.
If there are no stars in the sky,
Think !
What will happen?
The sky will become empty.
If there is no Earth,
Think !
What will happen?
There will be no life.
If there is no air,
Think !
What will happen?
We'll die.
If there are no clouds,
Think !
What will happen?
There will be no rain.
If there is no water,
Think!

What will happen?
There will be no creation.
If there is no tree,
Think !
What will happen?
There will be no greenery.
If there is no flower,
Think !
What will happen?
There will be no fragrance.
If there is no birds,
Think !
What will happen?
There will be no songs.
If there is no man,
Think !
What will happen?
There will be no civilization.
If we've no house,
Think !
What will happen?
We'll become nomad.
If there is no wisdom,
Think !
What will happen?
We'll become like animals.
If there is no love ,
Think !
What will happen?
We'll become like devil.
If we've no friends,
Think !
What will happen?
We'll become lonely.
If there is nothing in this world,
Think !
What will happen?

Everything will become meaningless.

……****…..

58

<u>Love</u>

Love yourself,
Love your mother,
Love your father,
Love your brother,
Love your sister,
Love your spouse,
Love your friends,
Love your relatives,
Even love your enemies,
And love every creatures of this world.
If you know how to love,
Then you know the art of living.
Love teach you everything,
Without love, there is nothing.
Love is the mother of everything,
Live your life with love.

……****…..

59

<u>Keep Busy!</u>

The Sun is always shinning,
He has full of rays,
Because he is, busy.
The Wind is always blowing,
She has full of power,
Because she is, busy.
The River is always flowing,
It has full of resources,
Because it is, busy.
The Trees are always growing,
They have full of lives,
Because they are, busy.
The Flowers are always blooming,
They have full of colors,
Because they are, busy.
The Ants are always moving,
They have full of stamina,
Because they are, busy.
The Bees are always flying,
They have full of sweets,
Because they are, busy.
If you're busy in your work,
You'll progress in your life.
Busy man is always happy.
Keep Busy!

60

<u>The Blowing Air</u>

If I were be the blowing wind,
I'll fly everywhere.
I'll try to clean the dirty mind.
I'll try to blow away all the stresses of mind.

I'll try to give fresh air.
I'll try to give lights of fair
I'll try to wash away all the worries.
I'll try to give the blessing of merry.
I'll try to give the ever lasting peace.
I'll try to give all bliss
I'll try to give cure,
I'll try to make all pure.
I'll try to give my heartiest wishes,
I'll try to give my loving kisses.
I'll try to spread the messages of love,
I'll try to sprout the blooming hope.

......****.....

61

<u>Born and Die</u>

Life is like a flower,
Sometime it gets the drops of shower.
Sometime faded with changing season,
Sometime blooming with new season.
It spreads her fragrance,
It attracts with her elegance.
Sometime the happiness of butterflies flies around her,
Sometime the sucking bees surround her.
But, with the setting of sun,
Everything will run.
And she will get down,
To sleep forever on the ground.
It's the cycle of nature,
Born and die are its feature.

.....********.....

62

<u>People</u>

There are many people,
Some are looking very simple,
Some are appearing very complex,
They have different perplex.
But, whoever you meet,
Try to greet.
Some may behave friendly,
Some may show their envy.
Not all are equal and same,
But, you needn't to feel shame.
You just pass your goodwill,
Without committing ill.
Our life is too short,
Don't make your blood hot.
Try to live in every moment,
With your great movement.

.....********.....

63

<u>Silent !</u>

Look at the sun!

How silently...
It is glowing.
Look at the Moon!
How silently...
It is shinning.
Look at the Stars!
How silently...
They are twinkling.
Look at the water!
How silently...
It is flowing.
Look at the air!
How silently..........
It is blowing.
Look at the trees!
How silently.........
They are growing.
Look at the flowers!
How silently..........
They are blooming.
Look at the animals!
How silently..........
They are moving.
Look at the birds!
How silently.........
They are flying.
Look at yourself!
How are you?
Are you silent... ?
There is only one way to live...
That is the way to live silent.

.......****.....

64

<u>Take Sometime</u>

Take some time to think,
Take some time to look,
Take some time to talk,
Take some time to walk,
Take some time to work,
Take some time to know thyself.
Let us allow the whole cosmos comes to you.
Feel the thrills of whole universe.
Take some time to thyself.

......****.....

65

<u>Yourself</u>

Think yourself,
Act yourself,
Look yourself,
Watch yourself,
Teach yourself,
Learn yourself,
Read yourself,
Recite yourself,
Compose yourself,
Sing yourself,

Work yourself,
Sail yourself,
Discover yourself,
Explore yourself,
Experiment yourself,
Find yourself,
Know yourself,
When you know yourself,
Then you find your true self.

......****.....

66

<u>The Blooming Flower</u>

The blooming flower looks very beautiful,
It is silent and serene.
It is innocent as a little child.
It smiles every time.
Whether hot or cold.
Whether rainy or sunny.
In every season,
It keeps her lovely smiling.
Whether it is growing in the garden
Or it is growing in the roadside.
Whether it is growing in the courtyard
Or it is growing in the backyard.
It never lost its magical charm.
Every time it spreads her fragrance.
It attracts everybody's' eyes.
The tiny bees; the colorful butterflies, and the small humming birds
Are flying nearby.
They love her sweet honey.
Its fantastic color changes our moods.
We feel joy and pleasures.

Even it melts the heart of a stonehearted man.
It steals the heart of every man.
It tells us the wisdom of nature.
It teaches us the lessons of love, compassion, purity, and kindness.
It is how nice, if the fragrance of flower is in the heart of every man.
And every time it bloom in everybody's' face.

......****.....

67

I Thank You !

I Thank You!
O! My dear Life.
Because,...............
You taught me the sweet taste of love.
You taught me the bitter taste of hatred.
You taught me the bonds of friendship.
You taught me the bondage of foes.
You taught me the joys of happiness.
You taught me the agony of sorrows.
You taught me the feelings of lonely.
You taught me the intimacy of company.

You taught me the godliness of divinity.
You taught me the evil of devils.
You taught me the journey to 'Death'.
You taught me the lessons to 'Alive'.
You taught me the true meanings of 'Life'.
You taught me the secrets of this 'Life'.
I Thank You!
O! My dear Life.

.......****.....

68

<u>You Can See.........</u>

In the rays of Sun,
You can see its energy.
In the lights of Moon,
You can see its calmness.
In the twinkling Stars,
You can see their friendliness.
In the standing Mountain,
You can see its strength.
In the flying Clouds,
You can see their lightness.
In the waves of Sea,
You can see their continuity.
In the falling Stream,
You can see its force.
In the flowing River,
You can see its smoothness.
In the leaves of Tree,
You can see their patience.
In the drops of dew,
You can see their purities.
In the songs of Birds,

You can see their devotions.
In the humming of Bees,
You can see their freedom.
In the blooming of Flowers,
You can see their smiles.
In the flying Butterflies,
You can see their happiness.
In the walking of Ants,
You can see their unity.
In Your life,
You can see love everywhere.

......****.....

69

<u>Love Yourself!</u>

Nothing can make you fly,
But, love.
Nothing can make you joy.
But, love,
Nothing can make you sad,
But, love.
Nothing can make you smile,
But, love.

Nothing can make you cry,
But, love.
Nothing can make you mad,
But, love.
Nothing can make you sing,
But, love.
Nothing can make you dance,
But, love.
Nothing can make you die,
But, love.
Nothing can make you alive.
But, love.
Nothing can make you complete,
But, love.

Nothing can make you feel wonderful,
But, love.
Nothing can make you live.
But, love.
Nothing can make you love,
But, love itself.

......****.....

70

<u>Why Not You !</u>

If the Sun loves to rise,
Then why not you?
If the Moon loves to shine,
Then why not you?
If the Stars loves to twinkle,
Then why not you?
If the Clouds loves to shed rains,
Then why not you?
If the Wind loves to blow,
Then why not you?
If the Rivers loves to flow,
Then why not you?
If the Streams loves to fall,
Then why not you?
If the Trees love to grow,
Then why not you?

......****.....

71

<u>You are born to be Wise!</u>

You're not born to be bad,
But, you're born to be good.
You're not born to be weak,
But, you're born to be strong.
You're not born to be poor,
But, you're born to be rich.
You're not born to be small,

But, you're born to be great.
You're not born to be low,
But, you're born to be high.
You're not born to fall,
But, you're born to rise.
You're not born to be slow,
But, you're born to be fast.
You're not born to hate,
But, you're born to love.
You're not born to be sad,
But, you're born to be happy.
You're not born to be impatience,
But, you're born to be patience.
You're not born to be pessimistic,
But, you're born to be optimistic.
You're not born to be failure,
But, you're born to be winner.
You're not born to be foe,
But, you're born to be friend.
You're not born to be sinner,
But, you're born to be pious.
You're not born to be ignorant,
But, you're born to be wise.

......****.....

72

<u>You've to Live Your Life</u>

Life is a shadow,
Sometime it's dark.
Sometime it's glow.
When the lights fall on it,
It shows its reflecting heat.
It shines as the rising sun,
And help you to run.
But, at the same time,
It gives you both tears and smiles.
The shadow formed in your front and in your back,
In the morning, it's long,
In the evening, it's long;
At noon, it's short,
But, you've to keep your life's cord.
If one side of your life is bright,
The other side of your life will be night.
Happiness and sorrow both are walking together,
You can't hold them any longer.
If the former gives, you delight,
The later gives you fright.
It's the part of your life,
But, anyhow you've to live your life.

.....****.....

73

<u>You're born as the Brave Soldier</u>

You're born as the brave soldier,
You've to walk with the tall shoulder.
Your foremost duty is to fight,
It's your right.
You've to go day and night,

It's your pride.
You've to reach far and wide,
With your own solely might.
You've a strong weapon,
Go on and on.
Clear your foggy eyesight,
Search your lost light.
Every time you'll face the deadly defeat,
But, you've to grip your slipping feet.
If you can, hug your death, which is your greatest fate.
But, never lay down,
Even you break down.
Never give up!
Raise your thumps up!
If you die for your motherland,
She will surely reward you with her blessing garland.

……****…..

74

You're the Master of Your Own

You're the creator of your own,
You can create anything.
You're the maker of your own,
You can make anything.
You're the discoverer of your own,
You can discover anything.
You're the inventor of your own,
You can invent anything.
Whether for your life or your world,
Whether for your nature or your future.
You can!
Believe yourself.
Nothing is impossible for you,
Everything is possible for you.

You're the maker of your own,
You're the master of your own.

......****.....

75

<u>Love is a Prayer</u>

Love is a prayer,
It's enriching when we share.
Love is a divine worship,
It mends the bond of friendship.
Love is devotion,
That changes one's life notion.
Love is pious,
It binds us.
Love is the only medicine,
That cures all our sins.
Love is the language of our heart,
That brings our heart to heart.
Nobody can live without it,
Love is the greatest feat.
Love cools down the fire of hatred,
And bring us the rain of sacred.
Love clears our heart and soul,
And build our house in the blissful world.

......****.....

76

<u>The Law of Natural Ordination</u>

Everything is runs by its rotation,
It's the law of natural ordination.
If you've a gala day,
Who knows tomorrow you've a cumbersome day.
If you misuse your power,
Soon you'll blow away like the ash power.
Everybody has own right,
Never hurt anybody.
Give your heart's regard,
Act as you're everybody's ward.
Whether giant or wee,
Whether he or she,
If you ever try to dominate,
Soon you'll eliminate.
Never try to roam like the insane elephant,
Else, you'll meet your the end.
A day will come when you'll fall down,
And no one will come to rescue your crown.

......****.....

77

<u>You will never regain it!</u>

Where are you standing right now?
How are you posing right now?
Look at yourself,
See your footsteps,
See your moving feet,
Change your outfit.
Look all around,
The world is not round,
It's becoming flat,
So, don't be late.

Now the world is becoming too small,
Everything comes too close,
And nothing is remaining old.
Peel out your sophisticated costumes,
Feel the new fume.
But, one thing!
Never forget your true self,
Your identity,
Your dignity,
Once you lost it,
You'll never regain it.

…….****…..

78

<u>In search of life</u>

In search of life,
I'm wondering hither and thither.
Sometime here,
Sometime there,
Whether I'd get my shinning dream,
Or I'd get mirage of beam.
I don't know.
But I'm on my way.
On the curving road of life,
I'm walking all alone even biting a sharp knife.
Every moment I'm facing test.
But I try my best.
Whether I'd get success or failure.
I don't know,
But I'm on my way
Into the cave of darkness,
I'm trying to get some brightness.
Sometime I'm getting hard knock,
Sometime I'm getting harsh shock.
But I'm on my way.

......****.....

79

<u>Under Your Feet</u>

Let the whole world laugh at you,
But never leave your self-view.
It's their reason,
But, never put-off your vision.
Maintain your own dignity,
Create your identity.
Keep your self-esteem.
Like the boiling steam.
Never beg for anything,
You're not born to sting.
But, you're here to rule,
Never become fool.
Go on with one mind,
Follow your own lifeline.
You've a mighty heart,
You're only here to make a new art.
Just you need to re-discover yourself,
To find out your lost shelf.
Then everything will be under your feet,
You'll reach in the highest summit.

......****.....

80

<u>You're a Great Soul</u>

If you've an ink and a pen,
Then you've everything in your hand.
Just jot down!
But never break down.

It's your powerful weapon,
Don't beg with an empty spoon.
You're very special,
You're not alone.
Don't worry!
Always be merry!
Life is not a blank page,
Turn it as a golden age.
You've rights to write your own story,
You've rights to make a new history.
Create your own book,
To reveal your outlook.
Tell the world
That you're a great soul.
You're bound to get your destiny

…….****…..

81

<u>Rub your tears</u>

Rub your tears,
Forget your fears.
These are the sign of your weakness,
These bring you unhappiness.
Forget your dreadful past,
Else, it'll be overcast.
You're here to become an outclass,
You belong to a special class.
If you run away like an outlaw,
You'll get a very hard blow.
You're not a coward,
You're here for your reward.
Don't do anything in hurry,
It'll brings you worry.

Be calm and patient,
Your Lord will bless you the grand present.
Don't make the house of glass,
Make it for long last.
You're in your creation,
You're in own destruction.
Everything is in your reach,
Just you need to become rich.
Go ahead……………

Don't be sad.
You're bound to get your destiny,
Even you're very tiny.

……****…..

82

<u>You're very special</u>

You've to open your closed door,
Even you're very poor.

If there is a doubt,
Even you've to go out.
You've to go...........
Even you'll face woe.
How your life will turn round,
When you'll get your rising dawn.
You can't say.
After every dark night,
You'll get the rising sunlight.
Everybody is born for something,
Don't feel that you're nothing.
Don't pause,
Your life is for good cause.
Life is to live,
But, not to die.
Find out your strong point,
To know your turning point.
Don't spend your life in dreadful cell,
Because you're very special.

......****.....

83

The Smiling Lady

Success never comes early,
You've to work daily.
Worship in your soil,
Even shed your sweats,
But keep your handy toil.
Anchor your aim,
Your labor never makes you lame.
Every day is your new test,
You're not born to take rest.
Don't afraid from the burning sun,
If you want your lively fun.

It's not easy,
It's not for lazy.
It takes time,
But it'll make you fine.
She wears her disguise dress in shady,
It's too difficult to please the smiling lady.
But she'll definitely smile you one day.

......****.....

84

<u>For Your Next Mission</u>

O! Crying eyes,
O! Dying hearts,
O! Tiring minds,
O! Sleeping souls,
Love your life,
Love your world,
You're the most lovable,
You're the most valuable,
Don't waste your beautiful life!
Life is all about hardship,
Life is all about worship.
Why are you be fooled by the self-created illusion?
Why you indulged in the bad dilution?
Come out!
Get out!
Stand up!
Wake up!
Do something for yourself,
Do something for all.
Be steady!
Get ready!

For your next mission.

......****.....

85

<u>The Little Candle</u>

In the dark night,
When there is no sight,
The little candle is burning alone,
Fighting all alone.
Without fear,
Without care,
Fighting with the wild wind,
Fighting with the mad black queen.
Having a thin wick,
Without feeling sick.
She doesn't know any scream,
She only knows her beam.
She sacrifice her life,
For the happiness of others' life.
She keeps her vows,
Even she keeps away her woes.
She doesn't know any curse,
But, she tells us to search,
The path of light,
And to feel the delight.

......****.....

86

<u>Never Forget</u>

Your life is not like an empty bucket,
Never fall in the dirty racket.
Fill it with great thoughts,

Don't drop the chain of blocks.
Don't grow the weeds of greed,
It'll cover your clean deed.
Before you would see the shinning sun in the sky blue,
Cultivate the moral value.
Never allow the sewages to stagnate in your brain,
Sweep your foul smelling drain.
Turn your two hands as the hard steel,
So that in your green field you could till.
Don't allow your iron rode to corrode,
Decide your leading route.
You're not born to get rust,
Your life is not like rust.
Wash away!
Blow away!
You've right to have your gold,
Never forget your life's gold.

......****.....

87

Mirror

Life is like a mirror,
Sometimes it shows you horror.
Sometimes it shows you good look,
But, sometimes it becomes faded with fog.
When you talk with it,
When you smile with it,
It smiles you back,
Because, it acts you to act.
You see left as right,
You see right as left.
But, it tells you the truth,
Which you actually suite.
You've many different faces,

That binds you with hard laces.
Find out your true self,
And try to come out from dark shelf.
It reflects your true-identity,
So, maintain your own dignity.

......****.....

88

<u>Don't Sit Down</u>

Don't sit down,
Don't look down,
Stand up!
Look up!
Keep your aim high,
Try to fly high.
Go ahead in your destiny
With single minded,
Don't divert your mind.
Concentrate in your work.
Don't measure your work with its size.
Because every work has its own importance,
Don't think about its result,
But do your work.
Whatever you want to do,
Do right now.
Never postpone anything.
Never forget that 'work is worship'
Then only you'll get success in your life.

......****.....

89

<u>Love is Music</u>

Love is music,
It composes in our heart.
It's sweet,
It's awesome,
Every moment it sings in our heart,
It's silently flowing in our heart,
Its softness touches our heart,
Its songs make us divine,
Its melody makes our life pious,
Its every node fills our heart with bliss,
Its every rhythm gives us the meanings of life,
Love is the universal song,
That sings in everybody's hearts.
With its music no one can live in this universe,
Because love is eternal,
Because love is our integral part of our life,
Without its music, our life is colorless,
It's only the music of love that makes our life colorful.

......****.....

90

<u>The Flying Feather</u>

Life is like the flying feather,
Sometime here,
Sometime there,
When it leaves the mother's body,
It doesn't remain anymore for anybody.
Wherever the wind blow,
It freely dances to flow.

It has lovely fur,
That swing with the air.
Where it travels,
It doesn't know its dwell.
It is soft and light,
But, its desire is to see the rays of light.
It is tiny,
It has no destiny.
It only flies,
But, sometimes it silently lies.
Sometimes it fall down,
And sometimes it sleeps on the ground.

……****…..

91

<u>Hunger</u>

It is the hunger,
Makes the man to go…..
It is the hunger,
Makes the man to run……..
It is the hunger,
Makes the man to chase……..
It is the hunger,
Makes the man to challenge……….
It is the hunger,
Makes the man to fight……..
It is the hunger,
Makes the man to grab………
It is the hunger,
Makes the man to thief……..
It is the hunger,
Makes the man to rob……
It is the hunger,
Makes the man to beg……..

It is the hunger,
Makes the man to sell………
It is the hunger,

Makes the man to work……..
It is the hunger,
Makes the man to labor……..
It is the hunger,
Makes the man to pray……..

……****…..

92

Like a Bicycle

Life is like the bicycle,
Its world is moving in the path of cycle.
It has two wheels,
That is revolving by the order of Heaven's will.
Human soul is merely a rider,
He has to go further.
So, he must know how to balance it,

Then he can ride it.
Because as he pedals it,
It moves.
But as he stops it,
He'll fall down.
With his applying force it runs,
And every spoke spins with fun.
It is made to ride,
It is not made to keep aside.
Our life is to live,
Our life is to view the greatest site,
But not to die.

......****.....

93

<u>Like an Egg</u>

Life is like an egg,
It's very delicate.
Even it's covered with hard shell,
Once it'll fall down from your hand,
It'll lose its life's worth.
It'll break.
You only get its broken pieces,
Handle it with your loving heart,
Hold it with your caring hands.
Hatch it like the mother hen,
She cares her loving dear.
She sticks herself day and night,
Even she forgets her delight.
After devoting her test of patience,
One day her young ones come out,
And she feels proud.

94

<u>Agony of Life</u>

It's the burning of flame,
Which has burnt my name.
I died before my death,
It's the tragedy of my fate.
Everywhere only the flashing of ashes,
I couldn't blink my eyes.
I need a little drop of water,
To put-off this terrible, shatter.
My heart is breaking like a piece of glasses,
No one is with me to stop my lonely clashes.
My beloved peers are in their fast asleep,
None of them is awake to peep.
My dream house burnt,
And I'm getting hurt.
My blood and flesh swelled,
And I'm bound to leave my dwell.
I've no more shelter,
My life is flying hither and thither.
Now, O my Lord!
Hold me in your blessing cord.
Save me from this dreadful agony,
And show me the life giving new destiny.

......****.....

95

<u>Wait for the Right Season</u>

Before summer season
There will be no heating of Sun.
Before Windy season
There will be no blowing of stormy wind.
Before spring season
There will be no blooming of flowers.
Before winter season
There will be no falling of dew and ice.
Before Rainy season
There will be no pattering of rainfall.
Before autumn season
There will be no shedding of leaves.
Before any season
There will be no season of anything.
Before time
There will be nothing in our life
Wait for the right season
To celebrate for special reason
With cool and calm
Without losing your heart
Then one day you'll see the right season will knock at your door step.

……****…..

96

A Blooming Flower

In every season,
It blooms with its colorful looks.
In hot summer season,
It resists the burning heat of Sun.
In cold winter season,
It resists the freezing cold of ice.
In dry autumn season,
It resists the welting of dry season.
In blooming spring season,
It gets the beauty of nature.
In rainy season,

It feels the falling of heavy rainfall.
In windy season,
It feels the dusty blowing of wind.
In every season,
It never cries,
Even in dry.
It ever keeps its smiling face.
Wherever it blooms,
Everywhere it passes a gentle smile.
Everywhere it diffuses its sweet fragrance.
Everywhere it attracts with its beautiful colors.
Everywhere it spreads its happiness.
In every season,
It ever appears attractive,
It ever keeps its beauty,
It ever maintains its purity.
It is a blooming beautiful flower,
Inspires us to live in peace,
Its every single petal gives us a smile of gentle kiss,
And ask us not to miss the joy of life,
No matter how many harsh seasons knock in our life.

......****.....

Life is action and reaction

Life is all about action and reaction,
When you give positive action,
In return, you'll get its positive reaction.
As much as you apply, force on anything,
As much as it reflects its force on you.
In the walk of life, you can't take break,
Because life is not a walkie-talkie movie that you can retake.
Whatever life will play with you,
You can't replay.
It'll never be back flow,
Because life is like a flowing river that ever flowing on its own natural flow.
As you treat with your life,
As it treats with you.
As you never deny that good deeds always give good results,
And bad deeds always give bad results.
Like a flowering plant always, bear beautiful flower,
Like a thorny plant always, bear spine like thorns.
What do you want in your life?
It's depend on you.
If you're in the search of gold mine,
You'll get its shinning gold.
If you're in search of coal mine,
You'll get its blackish coal.
In your life every small step will count,
No matter where you want to mount.
Your one right step will lead you at the doorstep of heaven.
Your one wrong step will lead you at the doorstep of hell.
Before anything going worse on your life's track,
Turn back your heading steps from its crack.
So that you can move forward,
Leaving behind your unnoticed footmark.

......****.....

98

<u>Good Things will come to you</u>

When you see good things,
When you think good thoughts,
When you say good words,
When you do good works,
When you meet good people,
When you act good actions,
When you cultivate good habits,
When you earn good hobbies,
Then good things will embrace you forever.
You'll never deviate yourself from good things.
It'll always hold you from bad things.
So, keep it in your life forever.
When you become good,
Everyone will be yours.
When you become good,
Everything will be yours.
When you become good,
Your life will become good.
When you become good,
Your world will become good.
Always remember that good things always follow good things,
And bad things always follow bad things.

......****.....

99

<u>Change Yourself</u>

If you ever want to read something,
Then read a book of life,
It'll teach you the wisdom of life.
If you ever want to learn something,
Then learn the art of life,
It'll adorn your life.

If you ever want to say something,
Then say a word of goodwill,
It'll tell give you the blessings of life.
If you ever want to listen something,
Then listen to a voice of your conscience,
It'll introduce you with the truth of life.
If you ever want to look something,
Then look a life of great man,
It'll show you the real worth of life.
If you ever want to give something,
Then give a word of love,
It'll return you a romance of life.
If you ever want to accept something,
Then accept a word of blessings,
It'll bring you bliss of life.
If you ever want to get-rid of from something,
Then get-rid of from your bad deeds,
It'll purify your life.
If you ever want to do something,
Then do a great work,
It'll bring you a great contentment in your life.
If you ever want to change something,
Then change yourself,
It'll make you a complete man in your life.

......****.....

100

Grow Your Life Everyday

As a small plant, grow every day,
To become a big tree one day.
Grow your life every day,
To become a complete man.
Grow your thoughts every day,
To be happy in your life.
Grow your knowledge every day,
To be knowledgeable in your life.
Grow your wisdom every day,
To be wise in your life.
Grow your intellect every day,
To judge yourself in your life.
Grow your work every day,
To do great deeds in your life.
Grow your life every day,
To live your life in prosperity.
Grow your world every day,
To spend your life in peace.

......****.....

101

The Wandering Seed

In the heart of earth,
One day a small wandering seed was fallen,
The blowing wind tried to blown it away,
But the mother earth embraced it in her bosom.
With the fertile soil,
It got the dwelling home.
With the envelope of air,

It got the breath of life.
With the golden rays of sun,
It got the energy to live.
With the purity of water,
It got the nectar of life.
The mother earth bestowed it all the nutrition of life.
And one find day a small green seedling was woke up.
Day after day
Its stem stood alone to mature.
Month after month
With the showering of rain drops,
Its branches slowly spread its arms.
Year after year
With the arriving of new season,
Its green leaves danced with joy,
It bears a beautiful flower,
And diffused its aromatic fragrance everywhere.
With its juicy fruits,
The thirsty wayfarers quenched their thirst,
And they lied down under its shady leaves.

......****.....

102

<u>Live your Life</u>

The world is around you,
Your life is with you,
Then why unhappiness engulfed in your life?
Happiness is within you,
Search it in your inner-self.
Don't go elsewhere for it.
Forget the ghost of your past.
Live in the host of your present.
When you give happiness,
You'll get more happiness.
Life is to live,
Life is not to die.
Count every drops of happiness
As your priceless gift,
It'll enrich your life.
Live yours every moment as your special moment,
And turn as your auspicious occasion.

……****…..

103

<u>Inspire</u>

In the time of your own despair,
You're the only one to inspire.
You're born to win,
But not to cry in vain.
It is very shame,
If you're living in dying aim.
You've to find your own source,
Then only you'll get your course.

Don't try to regret,
But, try to elaborate your own grade.
Forget the other's remarks,
Only search own marks.
You've to create your own ladder,
Then you become your own leader.
You're the best,
Be ready to give your test.
Set your own goal,
And try to get all.
Spell your charms of word,
As your strong sword,
Perch your degrade,
To find your secret.
Find out your weak points!
Find out your strong points!
Try to improve,
Try to prove.
Carry on!
Go on!
Success will kiss you,
When you know your own view.

......****.....

<u>Charms of Life</u>

In your life
Try to become a man of quality,
But, not a man of quantity,
It's a charm of life.
In your life
Try to become a man of wise,
But, not a man of vice,
It's a charm of life.
In your life
Try to become a man of vision,
But, not a man of illusion,
It's a charm so life.
In your life
Try to become a man of result,
But, not a man of insult,
It's a charm of life.
In your life
Try to become a man of duty,
But, not a man of haughty,
It's a charm of life.
In your life
Try to become a man of faith,
But, not a man of hate,
It's a charm of life.
In your life
Try to become a man of lion's heart,
But' not a man of chicken's heart,
It's a charm of life.